Busy]

A fun collection of read aloud poems for boys and everyone who loves them

By

Paula Walters

Contents

Dedication

To Ron, who has always supported my endeavors! You let me be me (no easy task!).

About the Author

Paula Walters is a lifelong educator who has enjoyed teaching children and teens from all over the world. She began her career by teaching Americans in middle school, then earned a Masters in TESOL and International Children's Literature that opened the door to teaching English as a foreign language to students here in America. Success has been measured by her students, having been acknowledged in *Who's Who Among America's Teachers* and having been recognized in 1995 as an outstanding English as a Second Language Teacher by the Ohio Department of Education.

She now resides in South Carolina with her husband Ron and her dog Forest.

When not writing, she sits in her screen room porch, where she reads and watches the beautiful birds of Sumter National Forest.

Author's Note

As a teacher, there was no greater enjoyment for me than teaching a child how to use and love the English language. Teaching them to read was definitely a major path that helped them arrive at that. This collection of read-aloud poems was written with just exactly that in mind. You are your child's best teacher; reading together strengthens your bond and gives both of you the opportunity to enjoy the adventure of words!

The boys in this collection of poetry are precocious! They have a lot of energy and a sophisticated vocabulary. The language is rich, and their adventures are fun. To help guide you through this collection as you read it out loud, here are a few rules:

• Where there is a comma, slow up at the end of the line

• Pause at the dashes

• When there is no punctuation mark at the end of a line, read right on to the next line.

And, most of all, have fun!

Reflection

I brush my teeth.

I comb my hair.

I dress myself, then

Into the mirror, I stare:

"Who is that boy?"

I ask with passion –

"A warrior in battle? A secret elf?

An inventor of marvels yet to come?"

"All these things and more," I reply.

"After all, I'm a boy, and I'm willing

To try and conquer possibility."

Some days I can ride my bike so fast!

The next, I talk with Grandpa about his past.

Yesterday in my dream, I swam with the dolphins in the sea,

And tomorrow, I will fly high and think the sky is me.

I am a boy, and I love possibilities,

The challenges, the everyday fun.

I am a boy with many more adventures to come.

Lessons

I don't know why the sky is blue.
I don't know how I lost one shoe!

I often wonder what makes the grass grow—
I often wonder what I know!

But there is someone who helps me learn,
He is playful and curious and makes my brain churn.

The time together is never a bore,
The time together makes us want more!

Then Mom says, "Billy, it's time for bed,"
I hug my dog and then play dead!

Tomorrow will be another day
That me and my furry pal can play.

We learn together, my dog and me,
Each day's a classroom playing free.

The Beanbag Chair

Have you ever jumped into a beanbag chair?
Taking a running leap, and then you're there
In a bag of beans?

I wiggle, I squish, I dart around like a fish!
Ah, the beans! Lumpy and so smithereens!

I just wish I had seen the cat. He's not happy
About where I'm at.
He had to move 'cause of where I landed,
And, well, you know cats,
They never take being "demanded"
To have to do anything!

Maybe later I will make his peace,
But only when all fun must cease.
'Til then, I am comfy, happy, and free.
In this beanbag
I am definitely me!

A Good Night's Sleep

Good Morning, child.

Last night in your sleep

Did you have sweet dreams of faraway scenes?

Did you get to visit Kings and Queens

As a child of noble means?

Or did you just sleep

And peacefully keep

The day's joy in your heart?

Oh yes, Mama, I did them all!

I saw Sir Lancelot at the Queen's ball.

And I climbed the mountains of Irish Kilderry,

And I sailed the oceans with Admiral Peary.

But long into my adventurous night,

I slept peacefully, without fright,

Because I felt the love

A day together brings.

Because of you and Papa,

My heart sings.

Playful

"I want to play!"

"You've played all day.

I'm very tired."

"Then I looked at mom and yelled, "You're fired!"

Mom and me, we have our tiffs.

Sometimes it leaves me feeling miffed.

She is a great mom—

She just has so much to do.

(How in the world could I make it without you?)

I knew my tempered mad had made her very sad,

So I went to her and held up my hand

For her to take.

"I'm sorry, Mom. I love you so.

It's just that play is my M.O.

I just think the time we share

Always proves that we're a great pair!"

"Oh, Timmy, you are so right.

I always hate it when we fight.

Sometimes I just have other responsibilities

And sometimes it removes my childlike sensibilities."

"It's OK, Mom."

Tomorrow is another day, when surely
My mom and I can play.
I'm glad I told her how I feel
Because to me Mom is everything—
The very best real deal.

Boy Synergy

I went into the room.
There was no one there–
Just Mom.
Who was she talking to
When she asked, "Why did I have boys?
Girls are much easier."

"Wow! I thought.
Do I not please her?
Are the girls really easier?"
She turned around and saw my face,
Confused and sad.

"Oh, honey, I'm very sorry.
It's just that boys are, well, you know–
Superheroes who chase through the house,
Inquiring minds who bring in a mouse,
Speedster boys flying on their three-wheel trikes,
Running in the yard too close to brother's bike.
All this makes me fret."

"Ah, Mom, you can relax.

Don't you worry,

I'll slow down, I'll quit the hurry.

The mouse will be put out with his pack,

And I promise I won't ever sneak it back."

"Justin, I hear you, and I hope that is so,

But being a boy, one might not know

That trying to contain all your energy

Can magically create something called synergy."

"What's that?" I asked.

"You, creating escapades of fun for your friends,

You, energizing the day and hoping it never ends."

"Wow! Who knew that boys could do that?

Thanks, Mom, I loved our chat,"

Sh! I must go now and find that mouse,

(It has lived a very long time in our house.)

I am off to make some ... "What is it called, Mom?"

"Synergy."

"Yeah! See ya later."

Swordfight with My Brother

I love to swordfight with my brother,
But when we begin, you should see my mother!
She looks scared like she just had a wreck,
But me and my brother yell, "What the heck!"

I step forward and stick him in the ribs,
And he jumps back and screams, "I get dibs!"
"What?" I ask.
Then he runs around and jumps on my back.
Next, he kicks me and grabs
My stack of baseball cards,

"No, you don't! They are mine."
"Sorry, brother, quit the whine.
We fought, you lost, and now the cards are mine."

He's right.
Fair is fair.
He caught me off guard
Like a gigantic, sleeping lair.

So he has my cards—it makes me sick.
I'll just sneak out only one pick—my favorite player—

From the stack, when he isn't looking.

He'll never know it because I won't show it.

I'll just keep it with my treasures–

Swordfight with my brother?

One of life's biggest pleasures.

My Sister

Why must I have a sister?

She's gone camping, and I haven't even missed her.

I have the house all to myself—

None of her friends giggling through the hall,

On their way to her room, as I recall

Saying stupid things, most of all.

I can watch whatever I want on T.V.

I've gone all week—no complaints against me!

It's a lot quieter, but I'm okay with that.

I've gone all week without one spat.

There's been no fighting about who lost the remote,

There's been not one time someone sipped my root beer

float.

Girls are so very strange,

I sometimes question, "Are they deranged?"

They talk on the phone sayin' things like, "She really wore

that shirt!"

And then there's talk of someone who is a big flirt.

They dance like crazy, gyrating on a stage
Pretending to be a star, hoping to engage
All of their fans screaming for attention.
I think girls are crazy, did I mention?

Friday night movies and pizza are coming up fast,
With her not being here, I'll have a blast.
The movie is one of my very favorites,
I'll kick back and truly try to savor it.

No interruptions asking about a scene,
No grabbing the pizza and standing in front of the screen.

I'll never understand girls or my sister. I am just so happy
to be a mister.

Food Favorites

You want to know my favorite food?
It kinda depends on my emotional mood.

If I'm content, I eat ice cream.
On happy days, chocolate is king!
One dip in a cone, all melty and delish.
Many scoops later, I've eaten an abyss!

But if I have a very bad day,
The food of choice is cheese.
You can stretch it wide, bite it off real mean,
You can twist it, pull it, and stick it in-between your teeth!
(Take that, you calcium chunk!)

But if my day is oh so average,
I like to just sip a favorite "baverage"!
Milk, cola, juice, or tea,
That is the menu for little 'ole me!

Good days, bad days, regular ones too,
The food I eat is always true
To what is happenin' in my life.

The choices of my busy days

Depend upon my mission,

(And maybe a close look at what is in the kitchen)

Most every day is a favorite food show,

Thanks for asking—now you know.

Day is Done

I must finish now. It's time for bed.
I've really got to rest my head.
It's hard being a "synergy" boy—
Kinda like being the "energy" prince,
Stirring fun up from the time I awoke since.

Being a "synergy" boy is no joke.
Lots of hard work and dedication,
At the end of the day, it's like meditation
That feeds your soul.

Good night, my friends,
I had a great day–
Remember tomorrow–

Meet me here
And we will play.
Games, songs, words, all fun.
See you later–gotta run!

CPSIA information can be obtained
at www.ICGtesting.com
Printed in the USA
LVHW081752211122
733724LV00010B/814